Legends of Hollywood: The Life of Olivia de Havilland

By Charles River Editors

Publicity shot of de Havilland in the 1940s.

About Charles River Editors

Charles River Editors provides superior editing and original writing services across the digital publishing industry, with the expertise to create digital content for publishers across a vast range of subject matter. In addition to providing original digital content for third party publishers, we also republish civilization's greatest literary works, bringing them to new generations of readers via ebooks.

Sign up here to receive updates about free books as we publish them, and visit Our Kindle Author Page to browse today's free promotions and our most recently published Kindle titles.

Introduction

Studio portrait of de Havilland circa 1940.

Olivia de Havilland (1916-)

"Famous people feel that they must perpetually be on the crest of the wave, not realising that it is against all the rules of life. You can't be on top all the time, it isn't natural." – Olivia de Havilland

Olivia de Havilland is one of the last few living actresses who worked during the Golden Era of Hollywood, but also one of the most decorated, winning dozens of awards over the course of a 50 year career. Among those, she most notably won the Academy Award for Best Actress for *To Each His Own* (1946) and *The Heiress* (1949), more than a decade after she got her start as an 18 year old in Hollywood. Ironically, de Havilland was in California in part because the young British girl who had been born in Tokyo stopped in the States for medical treatment.

Of course, de Havilland isn't well remembered for any of those accolades or other movies but because she played Melanie Hamilton in *Gone With the Wind* (1939), perhaps the most famous movie in American history. Although she was a veteran actress at the time, de Havilland's career hadn't progressed much since she started, and rumor has it that she eventually got the role after her own sister, Joan Fontaine, was asked to audition for the part and recommended Olivia instead. Olivia was ultimately nominated for an Academy Award for Best Supporting Actress and became a household name in her adopted country overnight.

Having been typecast in light romantic comedies before *Gone With the Wind*, that performance ensured de Havilland subsequently had a long, productive and versatile career making everything from Westerns and dramas. Of those movies, she is perhaps most closely associated with the enigmatic Errol Flynn, another foreign-born actor who was more notorious for his roles off the screen than on it. Before his untimely death, they appeared in several films together and became one of Hollywood's most popular on-screen couples.

Legends of Hollywood: The Life of Olivia de Havilland profiles the life and career of one of Hollywood's most beloved actresses. Along with pictures of important people, places, and events, you will learn about de Havilland like never before, in no time at all.

Legends of Hollywood: The Life of Olivia de Havilland

About Charles River Editors

Introduction

   Chapter 1: Reluctant Actress

   Chapter 2: Hollywood Good Girl

   Chapter 3: Gone With the Wind

   Chapter 4: The Ingénue Grows Up

   Chapter 5: The de Havilland Law

   Chapter 6: The Red Scare

   Chapter 7: The Lady is a Star

   Chapter 8: Paris

   Chapter 9: Television and Retirement

Bibliography

Chapter 1: Reluctant Actress

"The one thing that you simply have to remember all the time that you are there is that Hollywood is an oriental city. As long as you do that, you might survive. If you try to equate it with anything else, you'll perish." – Olivia de Havilland

Olivia Mary de Havilland was born on July 1, 1916 in Tokyo, Japan, but her father, Walter, was a member of the growing upper middle class in England. After studying at Cambridge and getting a terminal degree in English, he sought adventure in the form of taking a position as an English professor at Japan's Imperial University not long before World War I broke out. He later became an attorney specializing in Japanese patents and corporate law. Olivia's mother, Lilian, had been an aspiring actress prior to meeting her husband and had studied at the Royal Academy of Dramatic Arts in London, but she abandoned her ambitions when she and Walter moved to Japan.

The young couple had been married less than two years before Olivia was born, but there were already cracks in their fragile union by then. Walter was a notorious philanderer, even in the early years of their marriage, and by the time their second daughter Joan was born in 1917, Lillian was thoroughly discouraged with her husband and her marriage. To make matters worse, both the girls had severe asthma, and the treatments available in Japan were not helping them. Thus, Lillian insisted that Walter take her and the girls back to England. Her hope was that the gentler English climate would allow her daughters to make a full recovery.

A studio portrait of Joan, Olivia's sister.

The trip home to England began with a ship to California, and from there the family planned to take a train across North America to board another ocean liner for England. However, by the time they arrived in California, three-year-old Olivia was very ill. Lillian explained to her husband that they needed to remain in California long enough for Olivia to recover before beginning the arduous overland journey. He agreed to leave Lillian and the girls in California, but he insisted that he must return to his law practice in Japan. He did not tell Lillian that he would also be returning to his Japanese mistress, though she was probably all too aware of that too.

Meanwhile, Lillian soon realized that California's warm, sunny climate was just what her daughters needed, so she rented a house in Saratoga, a small community about 50 miles south of San Francisco. She may have planned to live out her life in what came to be called a "Victorian divorce", in which two people would remain married but live apart, but Walter had more modern plans, so the two legally divorced in February 1925. By this time, Lillian, with her lilting English accent, had found work among California's aspiring stars teaching music and elocution.

Lillian also found another husband in George Fontaine, who she married just two months after her divorce was final. Fontaine was a self-made man and the owner of a large Saratoga department store, but he did not get along with his stepdaughters, due primarily to his harsh parenting style. The girls reacted differently to his presence in their lives; Olivia drew away from him and chose to spend more time with her mother, but Joan, on the other hand, tried to win him over by pleasing him and even took his surname as her own. Differences over their parents planted the seeds of resentment and animosity that would bloom into full-fledged dislike between the two siblings as the girls grew older.

Growing up, both girls attended Saratoga Grammar School, then Notre Dame High School in Belmont, and finally Los Gatos High School. It was while attending Los Gatos High School that de Havilland became interested in acting, and at her mother's urging, she took classes in public speaking. She also joined the school's drama club, and from there she became involved in with the Saratoga Community Players, which led to her starring in the title role of *Alice in Wonderland* in 1933. She later remembered, "For the first time I had the magic experience of feeling possessed by the character I was playing. I really felt I was Alice and that when I moved across the stage, I was actually moving in Alice's enchanted wonderland. And so for the first time I felt not only pleasure in acting but love for acting as well."

A picture of Olivia de Havilland in 1933.

After de Havilland graduated from high school in 1934, she began devoting herself completely to acting, including playing Puck in the Saratoga Community Theater's production of *A Midsummer Night's Dream*. When she heard that Max Reinhardt was coming all the way from Austria to stage the same Shakespearean play at the Hollywood Bowl, she knew she wanted a part in it, but Puck would ultimately be played by a young 14 year old actor named Mickey Rooney, so that wasn't an option. Fortunately, one of Reinhardt's talent scouts had seen her in the Saratoga play and invited her to work as an understudy for the role of Hermia, and fate intervened when the actress who was to play Hermia quit the production to take a role in a movie.

This production was the largest staging of *A Midsummer's Night Dream* ever produced in America, with the entire amphitheater transformed with live trees and a wedding procession winding down the hillside. Critics loved the production, and de Havilland made the most of it, remaining with the show until it closed and then going with the troupe when they took the show on the road for four weeks. Eventually, she was offered the role of Hermia in the film version of the tale, and at that point, de Havilland had a momentous decision to make. She enjoyed acting, but she had never considered it a career option and had planned to be an English teacher like her father. Moreover, she already had a scholarship to go to Mill College. Ultimately, her love of acting won over, and as a result, the 18 year old signed a 7 year contract with Warner Bros. a few months later.

Chapter 2: Hollywood Good Girl

De Havilland in 1935.

"Yes. It was a stock company, Warner Brothers…they had two ingénues, one was brunette, and one was blond…and they had Olivia de Havilland, the brunette ingénue. Well that's how the casting went, you see. It was either the brunette ingénue or it was the blond ingénue. It was confining in that way. I had no real opportunity to develop and to explore difficult roles, and that was tiresome." – Olivia de Havilland

A Midsummer Night's Dream was released in October 1935, after de Havilland had already made two other feature length pictures for Warner Brothers. The first was *Alibi Ike*, in which she starred as Dolly Stevens, the love interest of the title character. She also appeared in *The Irish in Us* as the female member of a love triangle between two brothers, played by on-screen opposites Pat O'Brien and James Cagney. She explained, "Thrust into my profession without any training whatsoever, I had to just flounder and just find my way. It was an agonizing experience. It's like jumping off a diving board in the Olympic contest without knowing how to swim or dive, and I just had to find my way. So one day, I said to Jimmy Cagney, 'Jimmy, what is acting?' and he said, 'I don't know.' He said, 'All I can tell you is whatever you say, mean it,' and I thought that marvelous counsel. It is key. Wonderful."

Cagney

Neither of these movies received the reviews that de Havilland hoped would make her a star, and *A Midsummer Night's Dream* received only lukewarm comments, though the movie proved financially successful enough that *Variety* could note, "Question of whether a Shakespearean play can be successfully produced on a lavish scale for the films is affirmatively answered by this commendable effort...The fantasy, the ballets of the Oberon and Titania cohorts, and the characters in the eerie sequences are convincing and illusion compelling." Nonetheless, for a time it seemed like de Havilland might end up teaching school after all.

Like most actresses during the 1930s, de Havilland also appeared in a number of short subject films designed to get her name out before the public or to promote a movie she was in. The first, ironically, was about the making of *A Midsummer Night's Dream*, while the next was about the work that went into *Anthony Adverse* and was entitled *The Making of a Great Motion Picture*. In 1937, she appeared as herself in *A Day at Santa Anita*, joining other stars on a visit to the famous track, and she appeared as herself again in *Screen Snapshots Series 16, No. 10*, in which she was joined at a swim meet by her favorite dog.

However, Warner Bros. had one good idea up its sleeve by casting de Havilland opposite the dashing Tasmanian actor Errol Flynn in *Captain Blood*. Both Flynn and de Havilland were still Hollywood unknowns, and the famous producer Hal B. Wallis wanted to showcase them both in a way to make them stars. He just needed to see if the two could work together, and according to de Havilland, "I was called for a test, simply a silent test, just to see how the two of us in costume would look together, and that's when I first met him. And I walked onto the set, and they said, 'Would you please stand next to Mr. Flynn?' and I saw him. Oh my! Oh my! Struck dumb. I knew it was what the French call a coup de foudre. So I took my position next to him, and I was very, very formal with him because that is the way you were in those days. We had never met. We had never met, and we just stood there next to each other. Oh!"

Wallis

Wallis' plan worked, as the movie opened to rave reviews and was also a box office hit that laid the groundwork for the two to go on to make seven more movies together. For her part, de Havilland would later admit, "I had a very big crush on Errol Flynn during *Captain Blood*. I thought he was absolutely smashing for three solid years, but he never guessed. Then he had one on me but nothing came of it. I'm not going to regret that; it could have ruined my life." Two years later, the two of them reunited in a radio version of the movie played on Lux Radio Theatre in February 1937.

Olivia de Havilland in the trailer for *Captain Blood*.

Flynn and de Havilland in *Captain Blood*

De Havilland's next two pictures were both period pieces that would make her more well-known and add to the allure of her pairing with Flynn. The first, *Anthony Adverse*, was set in France during the French Revolution, and de Havilland played an innocent servant girl who grows up to marry an aristocrat. A series of unfortunate events result in the two being separated, with de Havilland's character betraying her husband by becoming the mistress of Napoleon

Bonaparte. *The New York Times* praised her performance, saying, "Olivia de Havilland, always an attractive addition to any cast, is a winsome Angela...."

De Havilland's next period piece was *The Charge of the Light Brigade*, a film inspired by the famous poem of the same name. Though she was again teamed with Errol Flynn and the movie did well enough at the box office, critics were not enthusiastic about de Havilland's role, with one calling her character Elsa Campbell "attractive, but thematically unnecessary." Ironically, De Havilland would later learn something that changed her perspective on the movie and Flynn: "He never guessed I had a crush on him. And it didn't get better either. In fact, I read in something that he wrote that he was in love with me when we made *The Charge Of The Light Brigade*. I was amazed to read that, for it never occurred to me that he was smitten with me, too, even though we did all those pictures together."

De Havilland in *The Charge of the Light Brigade*

1937 brought the release of a third costume drama for de Havilland in *The Great Garrick*. Like *Anthony Adverse*, *The Great Garrick* is set in 18th century France, and de Havilland played Germaine Dupont, the Countess de la Corbe, who was the love interest of the title character. Though not universally popular, *The Great Garrick* remains a favorite among a number of film historians. De Havilland also appeared in the comedies *Call It a Day* and *It's Love I'm After* in 1937. While neither film was particularly important on its own merits, the latter did mark the first movie in which de Havilland co-starred with Bette Davis. The two women found that they had a surprising number of things in common and went on to become good friends.

De Havilland in the trailer for *Call It a Day*

Bette Davis

By this time, de Havilland was developing quite a reputation for her portrayal of "good girls", which wasn't necessarily beneficial for her career because being typecast limited her options. However, she admitted that she preferred playing that kind of role to playing a bad girl: "Playing good girls in the 30s was difficult, when the fad was to play bad girls. Actually I think playing bad girls is a bore; I have always had more luck with good girl roles because they require more from an actress."

Nevertheless, she was about to earn her most famous role.

Chapter 3: Gone With the Wind

De Havilland's publicity photo for *Gone With the Wind*.

"If I watch 'Gone With the Wind,' I always find it interesting. I think, 'What's going to happen next? What's that character going to do?' But you know, you never really need to watch the films you made again. They stay inside you, always with you." – Olivia de Havilland

When a novel called *Gone With the Wind* was released in 1936, The book became an instant classic, selling a million copies within 6 months, after which it was awarded the Pulitzer Prize in 1937. In fact, the novel had such buzz that legendary producer David O. Selznick had such great ambitions for making a film out of it that he purchased the film rights to it before the novel it was based off was even released. That Selznick had the savvy to purchase the film rights to the novel before it was even distributed to the public reflected his love for adapting literary classics, but Molly Haskell explains that Selznick assumed a great deal of risk with the production:

> "It's easy to poke fun at the literary, and sometimes pseudoliterary, ambitions of Selznick, yet he could have lost his reputation as well as his shirt, could have been a laughingstock…There were many good reasons (mostly financial) that so few studios were eager to bid on the book, but there was one overwhelming argument in its favor: the generalized nature of the story, the very lack of historical detail with which critics reproached it, allowed it to speak of timeless love and loss, of family and romance, of a titanic struggle against national catastrophe that reverberated with all the struggles, past and to come, in a young nation's history."

Haskell's explanation alludes to the way in which, despite much of the film being set in the Civil War era, the film still had great relevance in 1930s America, a landscape that was itself struggling with many of the same themes explored in the novel, such as economic loss and racism. In addition, broad themes such as family loss and broken romances were captivating to any audience. Selznick's interest in producing the film may have stemmed from his love for the novel, but it is clear in any case that the plot was well-suited for the screen.

Selznick

For all of Selznick's literary leanings, it is also true that he was committed to transforming the text into a visual spectacle that made the film far from a mere retelling of the book. Alan David

Vertrees discusses how during the production of *Gone With the Wind*, Selznick balanced his need to remain faithful to the novel with his desire to produce a great work of visual art:

> "Selznick developed the script with one eye on [Margaret] Mitchell's novel (and on the public's response to it) and the other on his visualization of the finished film. Indeed, the preliminary design of the film—not only as story but also as spectacle and cinematic achievement—was in many ways as important as the script itself. Selznick saw *Gone With the Wind* not only as an adaptation of an enormously popular novel, but also as a display of the full potential of cinematic art." (xii).

The technical accomplishments of *Gone with the Wind* are on display throughout the film, as it was one of the earliest and most successful examples of Technicolor. In addition, Selznick hired Victor Fleming (who directed *The Wizard of Oz* that same year) to direct the film and the famed Max Steiner to arrange the score. As a result, Selznick was rewarded with a film whose technical virtuosity went almost unmatched.

To help build buzz, the men behind the film held the now legendary "Search for Scarlett." Smelling a prime publicity stunt, Selznick staged an elaborate plot to entice as many actresses and would-be actresses to try out for the part as possible. He was supposedly looking for an unknown to play the famed daughter of the South and debutantes rushed in from every part of Georgia, Mississippi and Alabama, but they clearly stood little chance against such women as Lucille Ball and Bette Davis, both of whom also made screen tests for the part. Katharine Hepburn asserted, "I am Scarlett O'Hara! The role is practically written for me."

Even foreign actresses were enchanted with the novel and wanted the part. One of them, Vivien Leigh, had spent nearly her entire career in Britain but came to Hollywood just to try to get the part of Scarlett O'Hara, as she would later recall, "From the moment I read GWTW, I was fascinated by the lovely wayward, tempestuous Scarlett. I felt that I loved and understood her, almost as though I had known her in the flesh. When I heard that the book was to be filmed in Hollywood early in 1939 I longed to play the part…" Leigh added, "I wanted to play Scarlett from the first time I read the book. That was in London when I was appearing in a flop play. I fell in love with the novel and I gave the rest of the cast copies of the book as opening night presents. I told them, 'If I ever go to Hollywood, it will be to play Gone With the Wind.' They all laughed and said I was crazy."

Like her future co-star, de Havilland was instantly drawn to a leading character, but not the fiery Scarlett that every other actress in the world seemed to want to play. Instead, she saw herself as the gentle Melanie, whom Margaret Mitchell herself would one day say was the true heroine of the novel. De Havilland explained, "Melanie was someone different. She had very deeply feminine qualities…Melanie was 'other people-oriented,' and she had these feminine qualities that I felt were very endangered at that time, and they are from generation to generation, and that somehow they should be kept alive, and one way I could contribute to their being kept alive was to play Melanie, and that's why I wanted to interpret her role."

Hollywood legend has it that de Havilland's own sister, Joan Fontaine, was approached about playing Melanie but turned it down to audition for Scarlett. The same legend claims that Fontaine recommended her sister for the part. Regardless, Ann Warner, the wife of Warner Bros. head Jack Warner, thought de Havilland would be perfect for the role, so Warner offered Selznick de Havilland, Flynn and Bette Davis as stars of the movie in return for the rights to show the picture in his theaters (at that time, studios not only made the movies but owned their own chain of theaters to which they were distributed.). De Havilland recalled:

> "One day, I came back from location....the phone rang. The voice said, 'You don't know me. We've never met, but I am George Cukor. I have been supervising the preparation of *Gone With the Wind*, and I will be directing the movie. We are in the process of casting, and I would like to know if you would be interested in playing the role of Melanie.' Well, I said, 'I certainly would,' and then he said, 'Would you consent to doing something highly illegal?' Well, I said, 'What would that be?' And he said, 'You are under contract to Warner Brothers. We have no right to ask this of you, but would you come secretly -- tell no one -- to the studio?'...I said, 'Yes. I'd be delighted to do this highly illegal thing.' So, I did, and I read the lines for George Cukor, and he said, 'I think I must call David,' and he called David Selznick and said, 'David, I think you must hear Miss De Havilland read the part of Melanie.'"

Cukor

Of course, there was still a very large hurdle to get over: de Havilland's contract with Warner Brothers. "Jack Warner utterly refused to lend me for Melanie…I called Mrs. Warner…and I told her that I would very much like to see her, and would she be kind enough to have tea with me at the Brown Derby, and she said, 'Yes.'…I explained to her how much the part meant to me, and I said, 'Would you help me?' She said, 'I understand you, and I will help you,' and it was through her that Jack eventually agreed.…Selznick had a one-picture commitment with Jimmy Stewart. So he…gave that over to Jack Warner who needed him for a film and took me in exchange.

Jack Warner

De Havilland in the trailer for *Gone With the Wind*

Given the ideal match between Clark Gable and Vivien Leigh, it may come as a surprise to learn that Gable had no intention of appearing in the film. Gary Cooper had already turned down the role of Rhett Butler and allegedly claimed, "Gone With the Wind is going to be the biggest flop in Hollywood history. I'm glad it'll be Clark Gable who's falling flat on his nose, not me." It was only through Lombard's urging that Gable agreed to take on the role (Harris). Gable was also the actor that producer David O. Selznick wanted. Always careful of cultivating his image, Gable explained his reservations about taking the role: "I found myself trapped by a series of circumstances over which I had no control. It was a funny feeling. I think I know now how a fly must react after being caught in a spider's web. Scarlett doesn't always love Rhett. It's the first time that the girl isn't sure that she wants me from the minute she sets eyes on me."

As it turned out, Gable was as suave as ever playing Rhett Butler, but he admitted it was a difficult role: "I discovered that Rhett was even harder to play than I had anticipated. With so much of Scarlett preceding his entrance, Rhett's scenes were all climaxes. There was a chance to build up to Scarlett, but Rhett represented drama and action every time he appeared. He didn't figure in any of the battle scenes, being a guy who hated war, and he wasn't in the toughest of the siege of Atlanta shots. What I was fighting for was to hold my own in the first half of the picture - which is all Vivien's - because I felt that after the scene with the baby, Bonnie, Rhett could control the end of the film. That scene where Bonnie dies, and the scene where I strike Scarlett and she accidentally tumbles down stairs, thus losing her unborn child, were the two that worried me most." De Havilland explained how she had to try to get Gable to cry during one of the scenes, "Oh, he would not do it. He would not! Victor (Fleming) tried everything with him. He tried to attack him on a professional level. We had done it without him weeping several times and then we had one last try. I said, 'You can do it, I know you can do it and you will be wonderful.' Well, by heaven, just before the cameras rolled, you could see the tears come up at his eyes and he played the scene unforgettably well. He put his whole heart into it."

Gable and Vivien Leigh in *Gone With the Wind*

Even with all the actors and actresses in place, shooting the picture did not run smoothly. For one thing, George Cukor, whom she and Leigh both loved, was fired by Selznick just before the filming of the famous scene at the Atlanta bazaar. Appalled, the women went to Selznick's office in their hooped mourning dresses and begged him to reconsider, but Selznick was determined to replace Cukor with Victor Fleming. The problem was that, while Cukor was considered by many to be a "woman's director," Fleming got along better with Clark Gable and Leslie Howard. He had problems making the women understand what he wanted in a scene. To compensate, she and Leigh began meeting secretly with Cukor outside of filming hours to get a sense of how they should portray their characters.

Then there was the famous childbirth scene. De Havilland was still single and had never had a baby. Wanting to know more than what she could read about in books, she began to prowl the wards of maternity hospitals, observing women in labor so that she could more convincingly portray Melanie's agony. In fact, the scene became so popular that a comical still was taken of her and Leigh, in costume, appearing to be "laboring" over reading Mitchell's giant novel.

There was also some speculation that the prim and ladylike de Havilland would be dominated on the set by her feistier co-stars, but de Havilland spoke well of everyone she worked with and defended the notorious difficult Leigh, saying "Vivien was impeccably professional, impeccably disciplined on Gone with the Wind. She had two great concerns: doing her best work in an extremely difficult role and being separated from Larry [Olivier], who was in New York." She had similar praise for Clark Gable, saying "Clark Gable was highly professional. He was a bigger star than we can create today. I was just a mini-star when we did *Gone With the Wind*. I was afraid to talk to him. People can't understand it now, but we were in awe. Clark Gable didn't open supermarkets."

Of course, in the end it was all worth it. *Gone With the Wind* is still considered one of the greatest motion pictures of all time, and the film has been mythologized into American culture to the point that Rhett Butler's final parting line to Scarlett - "Frankly, my dear, I don't give a damn." - has become part of the American lexicon. At the same time, there is a wide gulf between the love expressed toward the film by the American public and the relative contempt toward it exuded by critics. Alan David Vertrees discussed this dynamic, writing, "What are we to do with *Gone With the Wind*? The most popular and commercially successful film of all time, embraced by popular historians and journalistic critics while generally reviled by 'serious' scholars and cinephiles, *Gone With the Wind* stands as both a monument to classical Hollywood and a monumental anomaly." But no matter how much highbrow audiences might disparage *Gone With the Wind*, it is not difficult to understand the appeal that it continues to have on audiences. The sweeping, dramatic plot centers on the vain Scarlett O'Hara and her attempt to find a spouse. Set in the American South during the Civil War and the Reconstruction era, Leigh's southern belle encapsulates the decadence of the South in its declining state. Her character is simultaneously egotistical and unlikeable, but Scarlett also exudes just enough pathos to appeal to a wide audience. The film also benefits from having one of the most celebrated romantic pairings of all time, as Gable's Rhett Butler, a wild and wealthy Southern gentleman, is the ideal match for Scarlett O'Hara. Despite spanning nearly four hours in length, the plot has an almost unmatched ability to captivate viewers.

Gone With the Wind was awarded with 10 Oscars at the 1940 Academy Awards, an achievement made all the more impressive when considering the competition it faced. It is no accident that 1939 is often considered the greatest year in Hollywood film history, as *The Wizard of Oz*, *Mr. Smith Goes to Washington*, *Ninotchka*, and *Young Mr. Lincoln* were also among the famous films released that year. *Gone With the Wind* garnered de Havilland her first Oscar nomination, for Best Supporting Actress, and as such, she ended up being the first white actress to be beaten out for an Oscar by an African American, co-star Hatti McDaniel. De Havilland cried about not winning but also praised McDaniel and allowed that she was proud to have been there to witness her historic win. De Havilland also received critical acclaim for her role, with one critic praising her "gracious, dignified, tender gem of characterization".

De Havilland was only 23 and still single when she made *Gone With the Wind*. In fact, she was so focused on her career that she wasn't even seeing anyone, so when the time came for her to attend the New York premiere for the movie, Irene Selznick, David's wife, arranged for the popular Jimmy Stewart to escort her to the festivities. The two found that they had a lot in common and spent most of the evening enjoying each other's company. While they were still in New York, Stewart invited her to see some Broadway shows and accompany him to the famous 21 Club.

Their budding romance continued once they were back in Hollywood, with Stewart showing up to take her flying or out to dinner, and for a time it looked like Hollywood might have another famous wedding to look forward to. However, de Havilland was still a British citizen and her country was at war. She also felt that she could not focus on her career and a marriage at the same time, so when Stewart proposed in 1940, she put him off. Though they would continue to see each other over the next few years, they would never marry.

Stewart

De Havilland also became involved with the mysterious and eccentric Howard Hughes, recalling, "Jimmy had wanted to take me to a party at the (David O.) Selznicks. Howard had already told me that he intended to take me to it. I told both of them I couldn't go because I was terribly sick with a throat infection. Hughes insisted that I should go despite my 101-degree temperature. So we arrived, and who should be sitting in the bar but Jimmy Stewart, who was the single client of the bartender, who was Errol Flynn. We had drinks, and I danced for six hours and went home without a temperature."

Hughes

Chapter 4: The Ingénue Grows Up

"The life of the love interest is really pretty boring. The objective is the marriage bed. That's what the heroine is there for, and 'Will he win or will he not? Will they finally make the marriage bed?' It was obvious it would be the marriage bed, not any other bed, but it was all about would they in the end get together that way, and the route to the marriage bed -- and that was promised at the end of the film, of course -- was a pretty boring route. The heroine really heroined. She really had nothing much to do except encourage the hero, and at the right moment...and you can't imagine how uninteresting that can be, the route. The objective might have been different, but anyhow the route is very boring. So I longed to play a character who initiated things, who experienced important things, who interpreted the great agonies and joys of human experience, and I certainly wasn't doing that on any kind of level of a significance playing the love interest." – Olivia de Havilland

By the time *Gone With the Wind* was released, Europe was thoroughly embroiled in World War II, and though she had been raised in the United States and had never lived a day of her life in England, de Havilland was still technically a British citizen. This made for a number of complications in her interactions at the studio, leading her to follow up on her plans to become a naturalized U.S. citizen. She did so in November 1941, just weeks before Japan, the land in which she had been born, attacked the United States.

While working on becoming an American citizen, de Havilland continued to make pictures, and she completed her long string of movies with Errol Flynn with two Westerns: *Santa Fe Trail* in 1940 and *They Died with Their Boots On* in 1941. The former was the ultimate Western, complete with noble characters, historical references and the inevitable "cowboys and Indians" shoot outs. It was one the most popular movies of 1940 and remains a favorite among classic Western aficionados today. *They Died with Their Boots On* cast Flynn as General George Armstrong Custer and de Havilland as his wife, Libby. It told the story of their life together from their meeting to his death at Little Big Horn. Of course, the story was enhanced with many extra scenes and ideas popular among Hollywood directors during the 1940s. Ironically, the similarity between the casts and the settings lead to these movies often being confused with each other.

De Havilland's publicity shot for *Santa Fe Trail*

William Lundigan, Henry O'Neill, de Havilland and Flynn in *Santa Fe Trail*

With the entry of the United States into the war, Hollywood was in an uproar, as was the rest of the country, and the studios were in a hurry to make movies that would keep civilian morale up. As they did so, they also became less concerned about the quality of their pictures, so it's not surprising that following her experience making *Gone With the Wind*, de Havilland became increasingly dissatisfied with the type of roles she was being offered at Warner Brothers. At first, de Havilland tried to work out her problems within the system. She appeared opposite Bette Davis in *In This Our Life*, perhaps because she was seeing the director, John Huston, at the time. Though the movie was not popular among critics, de Havilland's performance was considered acceptable, with Bosley Crowther admitting, "Olivia de Havilland gives a warm and easy performance as the good sister who wins out in the end…" *Variety* observed, "Davis is dramatically impressive in the lead but gets major assistance from Olivia de Havilland…"

Next, de Havilland agreed to star in the title role of *Princess O'Rourke*, though she had made it clear she was tired of playing ingénue roles. The production turned out to be fraught with difficulties, as de Havilland fell ill and often suffered from low blood pressure during filming. When she was well, her co-star, Robert Cummings, was often away, forcing her to play out her scenes with the understudy. Charles Coburn, who played her uncle, was elderly and had problems remembering his lines, which led to an exhausting number of retakes. De Havilland had always prided herself on being a hard worker, but the combination of illness and aggravation took its toll and she began to show up late for filming. When things on the set got to be too much for her, she was not above storming off, leading the film to fall more and more behind schedule.

There were also problems with the Bureau of Motion Pictures (BMP). Established to coordinate movies being made during World War II, the BMP found much about the film's comedic treatment of those involved with the war effort offensive. However, by the time the BMP saw the movie, production was complete and they could do nothing about it. Thus the movie was released and the critics enjoyed it, calling de Havilland "charming as the princess—so modest, yet so eagerly thrilled."

Chapter 5: The de Havilland Law

"I knew that I had an audience, that people really were interested in my work, and they would go to see a film because I was in it, and I had a responsibility toward them, among other things. I couldn't bear to disappoint them by doing indifferent work at an indifferent film." – Olivia de Havilland

By this time, de Havilland was tired of playing "modest, yet so eagerly thrilled" heroines, and it seemed that the only good roles she ever got were those given to her by another studio. This became obvious when, after two years of making second rate movies for Warner Brothers, she garnered her second Oscar nomination, this time for Best Actress for *Hold Back the Dawn*, in which she played a school teacher looking for love. One reviewer raved, "Olivia de Havilland plays the school teacher as a woman with romantic fancies whose honesty and pride are her own—and the film's—chief support. Incidentally, she is excellent."

However, while de Havilland was nominated for playing yet another "good girl," her sister, Joan Fontaine, had also been nominated for Best Actress for playing a very dramatic role as a wife who is afraid her husband is trying to kill her. The two had been at odds with each other since childhood, and their professional rivalry was only the icing on the cake when it came to their sibling rivalry. When Fontaine won the Oscar over her sister, de Havilland behaved graciously, offering her a congratulatory hand shake at the ceremony. However, when Fontaine snubbed her sister's attempt, de Havilland, who always worked hard to behave correctly in public, was not just disappointed but furious. Her younger sister achieving the ultimate acting award before she did was simply too much to bear.

This Oscar loss marked a turning point in de Havilland's perspective: "So I realized that at Warners I was never going to have the work that I so much wanted to have. After Melanie and Hold Back the Dawn... Jack would cast me in an indifferent film and an indifferent role, and I thought, 'I'll have to refuse, I must do it,' and I did, and of course, I was put on suspension. Now, the contracts allowed that in those days. If you said, 'No, I don't want to do this part,' they would then suspend the contract for the length of time it took another actress to play the role, and they would take that period of time, tack it on to the end of the contract. So in May of 1943, I found myself with six months of suspension time."

One thing led to another until de Havilland was approached by her agents, Phil Berg and Bert Allenberg, with an idea. There was a law on the books in California that prohibited companies from extending contracts beyond seven years. By adding her suspension time to the end of her contract, they maintained that Warner had violated that law. They introduced her to Martin Gang, an attorney who specialized in corporate law, and after de Havilland met him, she agreed to allow him to file suit on her behalf against Warner Brothers. She became the first actor in Hollywood to take such a stand, because previous actors had simply put up with the practice, afraid of angering the studio bosses and losing their chance to work.

Eventually, de Havilland was put on the stand before Judge Charles S. Pernell of the Superior Court of California in November 1943. She had been warned by Gang not to lose her temper, as the practice among the studio's attorney had been to make those questioning their authority appear to be spoiled performers. In spite of his warnings, she still found it difficult to cope with studio attorney's line of questioning, recalling, "Oh, he was so wicked! Gimlet-eyed, and he would say, accusing me in thunderous tones, 'Is it not true, Miss De Havilland, that on such-and-such a date, you failed to report to the set to play such-and-such a role in such-and-such a film?' And I, remembering Martin Gang's instructions, said, 'I didn't refuse. I declined.'"

The oral arguments ended just before the holidays, and by then, she had been approached by the USO with a request that she come and visit American troops. She had a personal reason for accepting: "I had a beau. He was in Italy, risking his life making documentary films for the Signal Corps, and I thought, well, I want my December to be constructive in some way, so I said yes." She was actually entertaining troops in the Aleutian Islands when word reached her that the judge had ruled in her favor, but of course, the battle was far from over. Warner Brothers appealed the case and convinced every other studio not to hire her to make pictures. For a time, it looked like she might win the battle but lose the war.

The case went before the Appellate Court in September 1944, during which de Havilland was in the courtroom but did not have to testify. After the oral arguments ended, she left the country again, this time to entertain American troops in the South Pacific. She contracted pneumonia while she was away and ended up a patient herself in the hospital she was supposed to be performing in. She finally got back to Los Angeles in December 1944 and learned that the Appellate Court had upheld the verdict.

As a result, her case marked the beginning of the end of the studio system. By the spring of 1945, de Havilland was a free agent and could choose to make any picture she was offered. Not long after de Havilland won her court case, World War II ended, and her "beau" came home from the war. She and author/screenwriter Marcus Goodrich married in January 1946.

Of course, now that she was free to work for any studio, the question was whether any studio would hire her. Fortunately, *Gone With the Wind* had made her a household name, and she was popular among the families of servicemen for all the work she had done overseas. She was also popular among her Hollywood peers, who appreciated her standing up to the studios. More than that, those studios that were indeed interested in being honest brokers could appreciate that she did not attack the entire system but just one very flawed part of it. Other challenges would come in the future, but for the time being, de Havilland's career was safe.

For her part, de Havilland felt only pride in the outcome, and with the fact that the decision still bears her name as the de Havilland Law: "There really wasn't any doubt about the right decision for me to take, and one of the nice things I thought was, 'If I do win, other actors feeling frustration such as I feel will not have to endure that. They will take the suspension, going without pay of course, but knowing they will not have to serve that time again.'"

Chapter 6: The Red Scare

"I wanted to be what my high-school civics and history teacher thought of as a good American. That automatically involved taking an interest in government." – Olivia de Havilland

After her success in shaping Hollywood politics, de Havilland turned her attention to national issues. Shortly after *Gone With the Wind* was released, she was invited to the White House for a luncheon and met President Roosevelt. She was impressed with both the man and his policies, saying, "I began to realize he took initiatives during the Depression that saved the country -- and probably saved it from communism." With that, she joined the Democratic Party after she became a citizen and campaigned on Roosevelt's behalf during the 1944 election. She also joined the Independent Citizens' Committee of the Arts, Sciences and Professions in Hollywood to support his policies after his death.

At the same time, she was also concerned about the possibility of American liberalism being tainted by communist influences. She had read about the mass murders and slave camps in Stalin's Soviet Union and knew that at the end of World War II, the Kremlin had issued a statement in which it declared that the doctrines of communism and capitalism were so at odds that the Soviet Union would surely eventually go to war against the United States. Thus, when she was asked to deliver a speech on behalf of the committee in June 1946, she was appalled to see that it was riddled with what she considered pro-Soviet propaganda. She re-wrote the speech herself and used it as an opportunity to praise President Harry S Truman's firm stand against the spread of Communism in Korea.

She was also disturbed by what she felt was a certain censorship practiced by the group: "I thought, 'If we reserve the right to criticize the American policies, why don't we reserve the right to criticize Russia?'" De Havilland later said that her dislike of communism stemmed from the simple fact that it "stood for the overthrow of governments by violent force, not by evolution."

That upset me frightfully, and it was absolutely unacceptable."

De Havilland considered resigning at the time, but she was persuaded to stay on the committee by fellow Democrat Dore Schary. Instead of resigning, de Havilland took to trying to work her way around communist sympathizers on the committee, and she began working with others to try to write a statement publically condemning communism. She found herself meeting nightly with a small group of committee members who shared her concerns: "There I was, the only woman in the group, this little Brit trying to be a good American." One of the men that she recruited for her inner circle was her co-star from *Santa Fe Trail*, Ronald Reagan. She recalled, "I noticed that Ronnie made statements that seemed to jibe with what my small group was all about. So I said, 'We should ask him to join us.' Before that, I'd wondered if he was a communist, and it seemed that he wondered if I was one. We told Ronnie what we were about, and he volunteered to take on the writing of this declaration. He came back and read what he had written. I said, 'Ronnie, it's not strong enough. It's not strong enough. It has to be stronger than that or I won't accept it.'"

Reagan

Reagan came to the rescue just at the right time for de Havilland, who had begun to experience anxiety attacks and was getting paranoid that others on the committee were plotting against her. Hollywood was in the midst of a vicious labor strike that exacerbated everyone's tensions, and when she tried to discuss the statement, chaos erupted. She later remembered that band leader and communist sympathizer Artie Shaw approached her: "He said to me, 'Have you read the Russian constitution?' and I said, 'No I haven't -- and how recently have you read ours?'" Later, when Reagan's draft was read, things were "so heated and contentious that I thought, 'This is it.' I had fought long enough, and as hard as I could, and I resigned." Many other joined her, including Reagan. Unlike de Havilland, he would famously remain active in the political process.

De Havilland would not speak of her involvement with the committee until a dozen years later, and by then, the committee had had been "outed" as a communist front organization. Shortly after World War II, Congress' House Committee on Un-American Activities began investigating Americans across the country for suspected ties to Communism. The most famous victims of these witch hunts were Hollywood actors, such as Charlie Chaplin, whose "Un-American activity" was being neutral at the beginning of World War II. Eventually, everyone who had ever been a member of the committee was called before the infamous House Committee on Un-American Activities. While some refused to appear when called, and others castigated the committee and its mission, de Havilland felt that she had done nothing wrong and therefore had nothing to fear. She wrote, "I wore a red suit and I said, 'Please don't think that the color explains my political opinion.' The staff investigator was infuriated with that line and roared, 'Strike that from the record.'"

In many ways, de Havilland's experiences with the committee mirrored what was going on in the entire United States during those difficult years following the end of World War II. For instance, her beloved Democratic party lost their majority in the United States House of Representatives because the party was seen as being "soft" on communism. It would likewise lose the White House to Republican Dwight Eisenhower in 1952. On the other hand, de Havilland did pull the teeth from the organization by leaving it and taking the other non-communists with her. Likewise, many of those who were perceived as communists at the time are now seen as heroes opposing an oppressive system. And perhaps most significant of all, five decades later, her protégée Ronald Reagan would be hailed as "The Man Who Beat Communism."

Chapter 7: The Lady is a Star

"I think you have to have a very responsive nature. Think about anyone who reads a book. You visualize the characters. You become one with each of the characters. For a moment, through reading a book, you have the life experience of the character you are reading about. I fancy that reading gives you all of these extraordinary experiences that are helpful in understanding people. And that's true for a person without an acting talent. For an acting talent, it is a very developing thing." – Olivia de Havilland

Given all her controversial undertakings, de Havilland must have been concerned about the future of her career, but as it turned out, she had nothing to worry about. Paramount immediately approached her about doing a picture for them, *To Each His Own* (1946). This proved to be an excellent use of her talents, utilizing flashbacks that allowed the actress to portray a woman across decades of her life, from the time she was a 16 year old unwed mother until she was a successful business woman. When asked how she managed to play such a wide range of ages, de Havilland explained, "It takes empathy. If you are going to do a good job, you have to empathize with a character, either instinctively and through feeling, or intellectually. Preferably in both ways, but empathy is very much involved, of course." The role earned de Havilland her first Academy Award for Best Actress, and since this award was voted on by her Hollywood peers, it sent a clear message that she had a vast amount of support for the stands she had taken.

Universal followed suit by offering her the lead in *The Dark Mirror* (1946), one of the first films de Havilland made after studying Method Acting. Often called "The Method," or method acting, the approach is a combined variety of techniques used by actors to immerse themselves in the thoughts and emotions of their characters so they could develop lifelike, realistically powerful performances. The "method" in Method Acting usually refers to the practice created by Lee Strasberg in which actors draw upon personal emotions and memories to inform their performance, especially when physical and emotional details from a situation similar to those of their characters are available. While classical acting instruction focused on developing external expression, movement and mannerisms to develop a character, Method actors did the opposite, focusing on deep, internal components based in the sensory, psychological, and emotional arsenal of the human psyche.

Since *The Dark Mirror* tells story of a highly disturbed young woman, de Havilland met with a psychiatrist to get a sense of how she should portray someone with severe mental illness. Her preparation paid off, and de Havilland received critical praise for her work. According to *Variety*, "Olivia de Havilland, playing a twin role, carries the central load of the picture. She's cast simultaneously as a sweet, sympathetic girl and her vixenish, latently insane twin sister." James Agee wrote, "I very much like Olivia de Havilland's performance. She has for a long time been one of the prettiest women in movies; lately she has not only become prettier than ever but has started to act as well. I don't see evidence of any remarkable talent, but her playing is thoughtful, quiet, detailed, and well sustained, and since it is founded, as some more talented playing is not, in an unusually healthful-seeming and likable temperament, it is an undivided pleasure to see."

So effective was de Havilland in her role that she was next cast as the lead in *The Snake Pit* (1948), and she found a kindred spirit in director Anatole Litvak, who insisted that everyone in the picture visit several mental institutions and attend lectures given by local psychiatrists. De Havilland was fascinated by the treatment options and went out of her way to spend as much time as possible with the patients being treated. Litvak even filmed some scenes on location at the Camarillo State Mental Hospital in California.

De Havilland's interest in the treatment of mental illnesses dated back to her visit to several psychiatric hospitals during the war. She would later describe her experiences interacting with men who had suffered mental breakdowns during both training and combat:

> "I came back from this experience, and I thought -- because there was a great stigma to mental illness at that time, it was not understood, and families that had a case would never speak of it to anybody else, it was a true skeleton in the closet -- I thought, 'These boys, their families, how are they going to react?'...And then, of

course, The Snake Pit came along. That was wonderful. That was just after the end of the war, and here was my opportunity to do something about that. And it was a marvelous story, an autobiography written by this young woman who had become really seriously mentally ill, was institutionalized and remarkably was cured in a day when they had no drugs at all for treatment, but the therapy that they used then actually worked in her case…. That film, in New York, when it was released, ran one year in one theater. People flooded to it."

Not only was the movie a box office hit, it also won de Havilland a Nastro d'Argento for Best Actress in a Foreign Film, a National Board of Review Award for Best Actress and the Volpi Cup. She also received her fourth Academy Award Nomination, for Best Actress.

1949 was a banner year for de Havilland for another reason. On December 1, her first child, a son named Benjamin Goodrich, was born. Unfortunately, her marriage was beginning to unravel. Perhaps de Havilland thought, as many women of that era did, that a baby would bind them closer together, but if that was her plan, it did not work. She and Goodrich divorced in 1952.

Meanwhile, de Havilland would receive her next Oscar in 1950 for her role as Catherine Sloper in *The Heiress*, a picture that marked a new level of involvement in the movie making process for the actress. She sought out the story herself, which included viewing the stage version on Broadway and convincing director William Wyler to fly across country to see the play. He liked it and subsequently convinced Paramount Pictures to make the picture. Paramount paid the authors of the play $250,000 for the script and $10,000 to convert it to a screenplay.

The movie opened to positive reviews, especially as it compared to stage play. One wrote, "…the soft and pliant nature that Miss de Havilland gives to the shy and colorless daughter is much less shatterable by shock, and her ecstasies and her frustrations are much more open than they appeared on the stage…Thus her emotional reactions are more fluent and evident…On the whole, however, her portrayal of the poor girl has dignity and strength." As she changes over the course of the film and becomes more aware of her would-be husband's true intentions, the character becomes more calculating, with one review noting de Havilland "is spine-chilling."

Not only did de Havilland receive an Oscar for Best Actress, she also garnered a Golden Globe Award for Best Actress in a Motion Picture Drama and a New York Film Critics Circle Award for Best Actress.

Chapter 8: Paris

"You knew that the whole era of which you had been a part was coming to an end. Whatever replaced it would not resemble it. A pall hung over this city. I had to rethink my whole life in a place that was coming to an end." – Olivia de Havilland

As the 1940s gave way to the 1950s, de Havilland began to cut back on her acting and became very selective in her choice of roles, since each one took her away from her young son. This cost her the role of Blanche DuBois in *A Streetcar Named Desire*, and in fact, she appeared in only one picture before her son entered school. *My Cousin Rachel* (1952) featured de Havilland as a woman suspected of murdering her husband, and it garnered her a Golden Globe nomination for Best Actress in a Motion Picture Drama. It also earned her enough money to support herself and young Benjamin after her divorce.

In 1953, de Havilland made the painful decision to leave the United States and live abroad. She and her husband had divorced the previous year, and she while the court had granted her full custody of her three year old son, she was concerned that her ex-husband might try to regain at least partial custody. Thus, she moved to Paris to make it more difficult for him to achieve that, and she grew to love her new surroundings: "I found France a very refreshing experience. The French were just recovering from the war and the occupation, which was humiliating for them. The embers of their civilization were just beginning to produce little flickers of flame."

Not long after she settled in Paris, she received an invitation to the Cannes Film Festival, and while there, she met Pierre Galante, then the editor of *Paris Match*. The two married in 1955, and their daughter, Gisele, was born in 1956, but the couple would separate in 1962. A few years later, in 1965, de Havilland would become the first woman to chair a Cannes jury.

During the time between her marriage and the birth of her second child, de Havilland returned to Hollywood to make two more movies: *That Lady* and *Not as a Stranger*. As a female pirate, Ana de Mendoza, in *That Lady*, de Havilland was not the one who was rescued by the prince but the one who rescued the prince, in this case Prince Phillip of Spain. It opened to mixed reviews, with one critic commenting, "THE sad truth concerning 'That Lady,' which opened at the Palace yesterday, is that while the film is one of the most handsomely set productions seen hereabouts in some time, it talks itself right into the seared, sun-washed Spanish earth. Olivia de Havilland, not the ideal Spanish type by any means, plays the role of the love-hungry Ana de Mendoza competently. But she talks so! Everyone talks, endlessly."

In *Not as a Stranger*, de Havilland played Kristina Hedvigson, an older woman who marries and ruins an idealistic young doctor. Like *That Lady*, it was not very well received. She also filmed *The Ambassador's Daughter*, in which she played a young woman defending the rights of American soldiers to have leave in Paris. As one critic all too honestly pointed out, "Miss de Havilland, for all her grace and sweetness, is not exactly a girl…There could be more bounce to the picture if it were played by a younger girl." Indeed, by this time de Havilland was a twice married 40 year old woman with one child and another on the way when she made that picture.

After an extended maternity leave in France, de Havilland returned to the United States to make *The Proud Rebel* (1958), another B-picture that was unworthy of her talents. However, for a woman her age in 1950s Hollywood, there were few good parts to be had. Her next movie,

Libel, which was released in 1959, barely broke even at the box office. *The Light in the Piazza* was just as bad, though her next film, *The Lady in a Cage*, was more interesting. De Havilland played a woman being held hostage in her own home by belligerent thieves. It was a far cry away from the sweet and shy characters she began her career playing, but it was still not a big hit.

De Havilland still had one classic picture to appear in, *Hush...Hush, Sweet Charlotte* (1964), in which she played opposite her old friend Bette Davis. De Havilland held her own in the picture, playing a money grubbing relative cruelly taking advantage of a sick relation. Critics approved of both their performances, with *Variety* observing, "Davis' portrayal is reminiscent of Jane in its emotional overtones, in her style of characterization of the near-crazed former Southern belle, aided by haggard makeup and outlandish attire. It is an outgoing performance, and she plays it to the limit. De Havilland, on the other hand, is far more restrained but none the less effective dramatically in her offbeat role." Though the movie received a number of Academy Award nominations, none of them went to either Davis or de Havilland.

De Havilland went on to star in few more movies during the 1970s. Of these, *Airport '77* is the most memorable since it was the third of the very popular airliner disaster franchise. She also returned to period pieces with the medieval drama *Pope Joan* and *The Fifth Musketeer*, but it was in *The Swarm* (1978) that she gave her last memorable performance. When her character sees the bodies of dead children out her window, she gives what was later described as a "scream moan" that would be famous.

Some might have wondered why de Havilland never appeared in any French movies, and to that, she offered a very interesting, and humorous, explanation: "I thought that I had made great progress with my French when a grande dame said to me one day: 'You speak French very well Olivia, but you have a slight Yugoslav accent.' I suppose there were not parts in French movies for actresses with Yugoslav accents."

If the 1970s were unkind to de Havilland professionally, they were even less kind personally. In 1979, her troubled marriage to her second husband finally ended in divorce, and with both her children grown and living on their own, she was once again alone. After considering her options, she decided to try her hand at television, a medium that would allow her to support herself and catch a few more rays of the sun that was setting on her career.

Chapter 9: Television and Retirement

"The TV business is soul crushing, talent destroying, and human being destroying. These men in their black towers don't know what they are doing. It's slave labor. There is no elegance left in anybody. They have no taste. Movies are being financed by conglomerates, which take a write off if they don't work. The only people who fight for what the public deserves are artists." – Olivia de Havilland

De Havilland had made her television debut in 1965 on the Western series, *The Big Valley*, but her small role in that one episode was uncredited, perhaps because she did not wish to be associated with the medium. The following year, she appeared in a televised version of the Katherine Porter novella *Noon Wine*, broadcast on *ABC Stage 67*. However, other than guest appearances on a couple of variety shows, she was not seen again on the small screen until 1972, when she appeared in her first made-for-TV movie, *The Screaming Woman*. In this picture, she once again played a mentally tormented soul, an older woman coming home to recover from a mental breakdown. She claimed to hear screams coming from newly dug ground, but her family refused to believe her and a mystery ensues.

In 1979, de Havilland once again found herself playing in a period piece, this time in a small role in *Roots: The Next Generations*. Two years later she appeared, as did so many other older stars, on an episode of the TV series *The Love Boat*. She also starred in the United States adaptation of the Agatha Christie novel *Murder is Easy*.

De Havilland would appear in four other TV movies during the 1980s. In the first, *The Royal Romance of Charles and Diana*, she played the Queen Mother, Elizabeth. The tale was romantic and her accent good, in spite of her American upbringing. She then donned a hooped skirt one last time to appear in a small role as a Confederate nurse in the miniseries *North and South II* in 1986.

After *North and South II*, de Havilland appeared in her last major role, that of the Dowager Empress Maria of Russia in *Anastasia: The Mystery of Anna*, broadcast in 1986. This appearance garnered her an Emmy nomination for Outstanding Supporting Actress – Miniseries or a Movie, and a Golden Globe Award for Best Supporting Actress – Series, Miniseries or Television Film.

Two years later, in 1988, de Havilland made her final acting appearance in *The Woman He Loved*, a made-for-TV movie on the life of Edward VIII and Wallis Simpson. This time, de Havilland played an American, Simpson's elderly Aunt Bessie Merryman. For this role she was nominated for her last acting award, a Primetime Emmy Award for Outstanding Supporting Actress in a Miniseries or a Movie.

Following her role in *The Woman He Loved*, de Havilland retired from acting to care for her son, Benjamin, who had been diagnosed with cancer. He passed away in 1991 at the age of 41, and he was joined in death by his father, her first husband, a few months later. Following Benjamin's death, de Havilland entered into a period of seclusion and mourning that lasted for more than a decade. She rarely appeared in public and gave few interviews. For a while, it seemed that she might never recover, but as a new millennium dawned, so did her interest in the world around her, and she began to travel and appear in public again.

Though she lived on the other side of the world, de Havilland maintained many of her early

Hollywood friendships throughout her life. She and Bette Davis remained close until Davis' death in 1989, and she even appeared as a surprise presenter at the 2008 tribute to Davis' life and work. In April of that same year, de Havilland also traveled to Hollywood to attend the funeral of Charlton Heston. Though they had differed politically, the two had maintained a warm friendship since they first worked together in the 1940s.

The one person de Havilland would never be close to was her own sister, Joan. Their issues with each other ran too deep, all the way back to their mother's divorce and re-marriage, when de Havilland remained closer to her mother while Fontaine gravitated toward her stepfather. By the time Joan decided to follow her older sister into show business, their mother was so bitter towards her that she refused to allow Joan to use her own legal surname of de Havilland. Thus, Joan used Fontaine professionally despite the fact her stepfather never adopted either girl. The final break between the two came in 1975 when their mother died. De Havilland was at her mother's bedside while Fontaine was on tour with a play. De Havilland claimed that she sent a telegram to Fontaine telling her of their mother's passing and giving her the date of the memorial service, but the telegram did not catch up with Fontaine until two weeks later, after the memorial service had already occurred. Fontaine believed that de Havilland had not really tried to get in touch with her, and the two stopped speaking entirely. Fontaine died in 2013, leaving de Havilland "shocked and saddened" by her passing.

Though retired and living happily in France, de Havilland does emerge from time to time for special occasions. In 2003, she travelled to Hollywood to attend the 75th Annual Academy Awards, and when she came on stage to give her presentation, she was greeted with a 60 second standing ovation. In 2006, she attended a 90th birthday party hosted for her by the Academy of Motion Picture Arts & Sciences at the Los Angeles County Museum of Art. In 2008, she was presented with the United States National Medal of Arts from President George W. Bush, in honor of "her persuasive and compelling skill as an actress in roles from Shakespeare's Hermia to Margaret Mitchell's Melanie. Her independence, integrity, and grace won creative freedom for herself and her fellow film actors."

De Havilland and President Bush in 2008.

Of course, the movie that more than any other shaped de Havilland's career was *Gone With the Wind*. One of the reasons that the picture has played such an important role in her life is that since Leigh's death in 1967, she is the only surviving leading star of the movie. Thus, for the past half-century, each time someone wanted to do a documentary or retrospective on the film, de Havilland was asked to participate. One of the most significant shows taped on the movie was 2004's *Melanie Remembers*. Produced by Turner Classic Movies in honor of *Gone With the Wind*'s 65th anniversary, it featured extensive footage of de Havilland discussing the picture and her role in it.

Of course, *Gone With the Wind* retrospectives are not the only work de Havilland does. In 2009, she narrated a documentary on using art in treating patients with Alzheimer's. Entitled *I Remember Better When I Paint*, the film was debuted in Paris in 2011, with de Havilland providing a special introduction. Indeed, de Havilland remains very popular among her French neighbors. In September 2010, the President of France, Nicolas Sarkozy, made her a knight of the Légion d'honneur, the highest honor that the French government can award. In presenting it to her, he commented "…you honor France for having chosen us." The following year, she was invited to appear at the César Awards in France. When Jodie Foster, the president of the ceremony, introduced her, the crowd broke out in applause and rose to their feet for a standing ovation.

In 1960, de Havilland wrote a memoir about her life up to the point, and it was entitled coyly *Every Frenchman Has One*. It has long been rumored that she will be releasing another, more complete autobiography sometime in the future. In describing to one reporter why she feels that her story is so important, de Havilland expressed a surprising amount of bitterness, saying:

> "I feel like a survivor from an age that people no longer understand. I want to try to explain what the 1930s – the golden age of Hollywood – was truly like. People forget that America was such a different place then, not yet the dominant force in the world. I also want to explain how different the sexual mores of those times were.
>
> And to recall what it was like to be a star in the studio system. How you were a great celebrity but also a slave. How I had to present myself to make-up by 6.30 am and work until late in the evening. How I had to make five movies in my first year. How whatever private life you had left to you didn't belong to you but the studio publicists."

Then, with a quick change of heart, she responded with the same positive note that characterized both her public and private life: "I feel not happy, not contented, but something else. Just grateful for having lived and having done so many things that I wanted to do and have also had so much meaning for other people."

Bibliography

De Havilland, Olivia. *Every Frenchman Has One*. New York: Random House, 1962.

Higham, Charles. *Sisters: The Story of Olivia De Havilland and Joan Fontaine*. New York: Coward McCann, 1984.

Thomas, Tony. *The Films of Olivia de Havilland*. New York: Citadel Press, 1983. ISBN 978-0-80650-988-4.

Made in the USA
Lexington, KY
11 August 2016